RAVENOUS:
NEW & SELECTED POEMS

Rick Mulkey

RAVENOUS:
NEW & SELECTED POEMS

Rick Mulkey

SERVING HOUSE BOOKS

Ravenous: New & Selected Poems

Copyright © 2014 Rick Mulkey

ISBN: 978-0-9913281-4-7

Cover art: "Peregrine Falcons" drawn by John James Audubon for the book *The Birds of America* between 1827 and 1838

Serving House Books logo by Barry Lereng Wilmont

Published by Serving House Books
Copenhagen, Denmark and Florham Park, NJ
www.servinghousebooks.com

Member of The Independent Book Publishers Association

First Serving House Books Edition 2014

For Susan and Hunter

Acknowledgments

The author wishes to thank the editors of the following publications in which some of the new poems, or versions of them, first appeared: *Poet Lore*: "Cheese," *Serving House Journal*: "Betrayal," *Shenandoah*: "Hunger Ghazal," *The South Carolina Review*: "Killing," and "The Monsters of Bomarzo," and *Runnin' Around: The Serving House Book of Infidelity*: "Desire," "Hummingbird," "In the Strip Clubs of Bluefield, WV," and "September." The selected poems in this volume appeared in *Before the Age of Reason* (Pecan Grove Press), *Bluefield Breakdown* (Finishing Line Press), and *Toward Any Darkness* (Word Press). My thanks to those editors and to the editors of the following journals where the selected poems originally appeared: *Bluestone Review, The Charlotte Poetry Review, Connecticut Review, Crab Orchard Review, Denver Quarterly, Emrys Journal, The Literary Review, North Dakota Quarterly, Poetry East, Poet Lore, Shenandoah, The South Carolina Review, The Southern Poetry Review,* and *Talking River Review*.

My thanks to Susan Tekulve, Robert Olmstead, Denise Duhamel, Anita Skeen, Susan Ludvigson, Kay Byer, and Albert Goldbarth for their friendship and many years of support and belief in my work. Thanks to Angela, Tom, Nancy and Aly for the supportive words and deeds. My thanks to Hunter for the music. And lastly, my thanks to Thomas E. Kennedy and Walter Cummins, two of the great literary citizens of our day, for their keen eyes, constant support, and loyal friendship.

Contents

I. New Poems

II. Selected Poems 1990-2007

I. New Poems

Cove Creek Catechism

Why, even after I've abandoned it to some unused cabinet,
do I hold on to creek-side flint chipped to shape a plaything
for a child? Mock artifact, this creek's ancient falls

can dredge up a thousand of its kind. Like prayer, water is a mystery
we can enter and leave at will. One moment we're the creek's
clear hymn, graceful ostinatos of rushing notes, the next
we're dull flint water-sharpened until it cuts.

O communion of tangled line, litany of roiling brook,
sacred text of fish-scale, direct this torn flesh, suffer it to recall.

Betrayal

Awake all night with the weight of age
on my back and neck, dragging my head
through the muck of a migraine, I look up
from my deckchair into sweet gum and pin oak
laced with dawn. Even here there are degrees
of darkness on the leaves. The neighbor,
an early riser, hidden behind the sheen of camellia,
whistles uncommon songs in his garden.
They are not of love lost or found,
or pain recalled, not songs
like that. They make sense only to him
and to his hound dreaming on the porch.
I think of the promise of blackberries,
how in summer drought they grow so tight,
dark and small, ripen with so much heat they taste
of the bitterness and disappointment of clay.
I think how we all want the rain
to touch our skin, how, as kids, our hands
wet after the storm touched the bark
of apple and elm, how we waded through fields,
bristled at the bearded chins of thistle.
We always begin to love the world
through our bodies. Each seed entering us
becomes us. Pears and plums along the stream
where young fathers fish for trout. Their lean
arms casting the line accept the wind gracefully.
Mothers raise their round smooth faces like blossoms
toward the sun. In their beds at night they dream their bodies
are the ancient fire original light sparked from.
This is why the body's betrayal
is so severe. The meadow understood

the river would wear it away. The morning glory
knew dusk must peel its petals off.
The child's body, naked and glistening in the lake,
expected always to be loved by the gods.

Hunger Ghazal

Even lonelier than the owl's question is the whisper of boiling water.
On the table, morning's cracked cup petitions its boiling water.

I wake to the root-bared light of November. While oaks shed
to reveal their truer selves, fog rises from my kettle of toiling water.

False summer, and the honeybee refuses the machinery of bloom and rot.
She sucks out life to form another: black tea transforming boiling water.

As a child, I saw rabbits after the flood spoil in the sun, crucified on briars
in creek side thickets. Empires of flies rose to profit beside the roiling water.

Of course there is the other, the teenage boy who spies the hips of housewives,
each daughters' sprouting breasts. Desire beaded on his lip, a kind of holy water.

My wife adds salted pork to the soup pot's steeped delicacies. Our hands brush gently,
as if again we're young lovers walking above the river's rolling water.

To look at us, you'd think we'd been happy all our lives. How much
our joy depends on love as bearable hunger, a pot of boiling water.

Music Theory

Down the hall, a young man, my son, plays bass
with so much passion the framed family portraits
in the room beneath his grind against walls.
Where does such happiness come from,
this sacrament of dance and thumping chest?
If I could, I'd stockpile it in coopered casks.
Each morning I'd sip from it, satisfying as August rains.
I'd spend my day in sun-laced gardens observing stones,
the simple pleasures found mapping the flight of bees
or the underground freeways of moles, evidence
the underworld is more than darkness and blight,
that Orpheus didn't look back in doubt, but in amazement,
that even in the soul's grim mines, one tuned string
perfectly plucked could make us believe all would be right.

Belly

Do not ye yet understand, that whatsoever entereth in at the mouth goeth into the belly… Matthew 15:17

Hunger is insolent, and will be fed. Homer

This belly is not just any belly. This belly is glorious
flesh rising on the east wind, cumulus over the Nile.

This belly is indiscriminate, full of ligament
and tendon, muscle and bone.

This belly desires grand ballrooms
to waltz, oceans to swim, galaxies to soar.

This belly warps space and time.
It is the event horizon, the devourer of stars.

This belly goes where it wants to go, says what it wants to say.
It is the alpha and omega, shaping the world in its own image.

Satiated on dates and honey, this belly lingers over Mesopotamia,
charts desert campaigns from beneath olive branches.

This belly is full of possibility. This belly is empty-headed.
This belly doesn't know what's good for it.

This belly is heedless, careless, impulsive. Working overtime
while others sleep, it's barely hanging on.

This belly cries no, no, no, but means yes, yes, yes.
This belly won't be stopped, slowed down, or knocked off track.

This belly hurries toward you with a gleam in its eye.
It takes all it can and still isn't sated.

This belly asks no questions, has no guilt.
This belly answers only to itself.

This belly is empire, is manifest destiny.
It is pregnant with its own survival.

What Superman Feared Most

Was Kryptonite, and, when exposed,
how flaccid it left him, no superpowers
for aiding Lois Lane, no rippling
alien pectorals for swooping in
to save the day. But nothing more.
My worst fear is that I have too many
to narrow down to one.
When I go to bed I'm afraid
I won't sleep. When I sleep
I dream I won't wake.
When I wake, I'm afraid the day
will bring bad news, the illness
of a friend, an oven accident
at the local Sunbeam bakery,
or a glitch in my new car
that forces me to waste the day
at a garage or discover just as I'd feared,
the model I was talked into by the salesman
who pulled his best Dick Cheney
end-of-the-world speech and convinced me
if I didn't have this vehicle,
I might not live to regret it, really was a lemon.
Or I'm afraid the day will bring good news,
the kind I worry I don't deserve,
news that reminds me of how shitty
all the other days leading to this one have been.
The kind of day you know can never happen
again, no matter how well you live your life.
So I hope I won't hear
any good news, then I start to think
how crazy that is and that maybe
the wiccan I'd lived with years ago,

the one who packed her crystals and bells,
and left because she swore I could never be happy,
that it was a waste of her time
to think I could find peace, was right.
I start to worry I'll always freeze in horror
when the furnace clangs on at night,
that I'll grow nauseous every time I open
my email, afraid of what message lurks there,
that I'll continue to rush outside in thunderstorms
to hold a golf umbrella
above the heirloom tomato I've tended all summer,
more afraid of the hail that will ravage it
down to empty stalks than I am
of the lightning carving up the sky.
And who can say why I'm not afraid
of lightning, something most everyone
with any sense fears. Maybe because
as a kid I wanted to be Captain Marvel,
the character who is often misnamed Shazam
for the phrase that Billy Batson uttered
before transforming with a clap of thunder
into the cape wearing super hero
with a lightning bolt across his chest.
Maybe the real fear is knowing
none of us can be Superman
or Captain Marvel with their super strength
and super courage, their abilities to outrun
a speeding bullet, leap tall buildings,
or, when the moment requires it, stand up
in the presence of Kryptonite, or Lois Lane, no matter the risk.
Sure, we could be Batman, but who wants
to be the caped crusader hopped up on vengeance.
It's hard enough revealing who we are
when to do so means fighting forces

in our secret selves we can't admit.
It's true, for instance, I've cried more than once,
especially at my son's birth, strangers around,
his mother exhausted, asleep. Yes, I wept.
I held him. I promised him a great many things.
But what can I tell him now,
or any of you for that matter, about those times
we all know, when we arrive home late
at the pissy end of a day spent
mining the rich veins of weakness and betrayal,
chiseling out huge blocks of shame
until our hands and arms, scraped and festered,
are filled, the chest crushed with the weight,
so that to move, to breathe, to offer up
one more fake smile is an act of superhuman strength?
How many times have I woke to find all I want
is to punch the world swiftly in its squared,
good-guy Clark Kent jaw. Yet, I remember
when my son was four and I arrived
at the school playground to find him on his back,
crushed by the class bully, heavy as any fragment
of Kryptonite. I was ready to help,
swoop in and save the day,
but by the time I reached him
in the sweat and dirt, he looked relieved
at last to recognize the salty-sweet taste
of his own blood, to scope the flesh of his wound,
to understand no one can stop the world from dissolving,
keep us from winds grinding patiently
at our secret fortresses and chambers.

Cheese

I'm not talking about the ones
threaded with veins of blue,
a living circulatory system of mold,
or the ones ripe with the pungency
of post-coital sweat. Those weren't for us.
Not then. I'm thinking of the big blocks
shaped like Egyptian mud bricks fashioned
with straw and blood, the ones
my father waited in line to receive
from the backs of trucks in that lean year,
the strike year, the year of brown beans
and cornbread, the year when a hunk
of poorly aged cheddar toasted
between day old bread on a buttered griddle
was luxury beyond compare.
In those months my father stood
sign-in-hand in the picket line every day
asking for little more than his fair shake.
Every day, that is, except the first Thursday
of the month when he'd wait his turn
behind the welfare truck for powdered milk
and a block of processed American.
Cheese, even the way the vowels stretched
across the ear, the way it whispered the lie
of "ease" into the air sounded like shame.
Even now, sometimes a small gesture is all it takes.
The way my neighbor, Mr. Local-Big-Shot,
Mr. Raised-to-Take-Over-the-Family-Business,
Mr. My Way or the Highway,
eating aged Kobe beef for his 4th of July feast
piles a mound of Roquefort on his slightly rare,

and flirts with the caterer's assistant, a young Latina.
She hustles from guest-to-guest
with a quick smile, performing her obliging dance
of foot shuffle and head nod, hardly noticed,
and taking, when she thinks no one is watching,
a couple of hunks that the guests won't touch,
of the processed cheddar stabbed with a toothpick,
nibbling like a little mouse
around the edges of appetite.

When You've Reached Your Limit

You may not know it, but
even before your first breath
a number existed for your last.
This is what you consider as you crawl
deep inside Aramark Uniform's industrial washer.
You've been chosen because you're sixteen
and the smallest and the one
least likely to complain. Of course, no one
would care if you did complain. The men
who work this job for real wages
have no interest in you. They know you
can't imagine their lives, you who take
on a summer job for date money, "pussy money,"
they call it. You who fill your Mustang's tank
with premium and shop the new mall
instead of Dollar General. What could you know
of work, of the ache of driving home
to a wife afraid of the sound of your key
in the door, a woman who fidgets beneath you
in bed like a bottle fly before a rising swatter?
Nothing. And nothing is what you know
of industrial washing machines,
yet you've slipped inside its stainless steel
drum and eased your hand into the small crevice
searching for the object, a key chain, loose bolt,
or name tag that's jammed up the works. It's hot in there
and tighter than you'd imagined. You begin to consider
how your hand could catch, or the cylinder might shift
and wrench your fingers from their joints.
You suspect this would change your life,
a man no longer whole. You imagine all the dreams

you had for yourself growing dimmer
and the weight of that thought presses on your chest
until you find it hard to breath. The men are laughing now,
punching buttons on the washers beside you.
They can hear you squirm in the guts of the machine,
and when you yell, "Shut the hell up, will ya,"
they laugh harder, not because they are cruel,
or because they can't stand you or your kind,
but because they know, like them, when you wake
tomorrow you'll think of calling in sick,
of staying home to do nothing but watch
the Weather Channel and eat leftovers
from a zip lock bag, but you'll rise anyway,
dress, drive twenty minutes to the edge of town,
punch your time card, its metallic click
stamping you as approved for this life,
because this is what it means to be a man,
so many mouthfuls of air, so many cups of coffee,
so many lunch break Salems and ham and cheese on rye,
so many mornings when you wake at 3:00 a.m.
to realize there is nothing else to do but move,
nothing else to do but breathe.

Earning a Living

As if being born, scrambling down
the birth canal and breaking free
of the wrapped cord and the false
safety of the womb wasn't enough,
we have to go out and earn it
all over again each and every day.

This is crazy. And my cat, Frank,
who has at least six lives left,
all quite comfortable, if he could speak
or be troubled enough to wake
from his nap or interrupt his 11th meal
to be worried with telling me anything,
would confirm this is crazy.

Yet, we all punch some kind
of clock, fill out another form,
personalize our cubicle with framed
snapshots of little Johnny and lovely Jenny
before the orthodonture broke the bank,
before the wedding reception
meant a second mortgage.

We're all heading for our own
mechanical breakdown. Listen to the knee
grind in the socket, the back crack,
the migraine scratch at the walls of the skull.
We're a blood pressure spike away
from a shutdown of the plant
and a permanent layoff.

And who wants to earn this anyway?
Most of us couldn't give our lives away
no matter the incentives we'd toss in:
the first dates, the first sex, or even the last,
the first hard drink, which really was the start
of one too many anyhow. Who'd want it?
Left overnight at the curb, who'd steal it?

Earning a living? What smug ass
came up with that phrase? Some silver
spoon holding, three minute egg cracking,
trust fund loving son-of-a-bitch? Probably not.
Likely, it was some poor schmuck who'd grown
tired of toast and black coffee and thought
a three minute egg might be worth earning a living.

Some decent Joe who imagined he'd be more
than a bill of sale, or a safe unlocked
at death releasing into the universe
a billion atom-sized Joes, spare change
tossed into a cosmic fountain. And that's why
most mornings I wake to hope
my life will at least fit

through the space of my cat's door
and isn't, as I often dream, as insignificant
as the abandoned "Whopper" wrapper
in the back seat of a Corolla. At least
the cat's door is always there, I think.
Then pour a cup of coffee and make some toast.

September

September is the syntax of pick and shovel
in the Tazewell quarry of my youth, the auger
burrowed out of sight, money in a young man's pocket,
and after work, the honking horn at the gate.
It is the homecoming queen rising slowly
from her backyard swing, knowing she'll make him wait.
It is the distraction of rain in the middle of the night,
and the moth's jazzy susurration beneath a porch light.
It is the fragrance of girls fashioned into women,
the smell of late night love in a Dodge,
the bittersweet blooming of dawns
that always arrive. How sunlight those mornings
is the one grief we never forget.

Hummingbird

Imagine each liqueur-soaked rose as a potential love affair
on this capricious tour of blossom-scented air.

Wings in constant flight, he reveals himself
as stained glass let loose to glaze summer air.

He lives in the moments between inhale
and exhale, between hawk-shadow and sun-laced air.

Imagine the stamen encased in a drop of rain, carnal thrum
of wind in poplars whispering to the pollen stained air,

we all fail love. Watch how easily he turns from rose to heather,
the way, as children, we'd practice our flying from the top stair,

choosing opportunity over safety, flapping our arms desperately,
believing we could abandon our solid selves, hover as light and air.

In Dispraise of Onions

I've had friends who loved them sliced between Wonder bread,
and others who thought it kin to blasphemy to leave one off a burger.

There are wilderness survivors who lived on wild ones alone. I couldn't.
Their layered hearts are always bitter, and if they're not

eaten by season's end they multiply come spring without remorse.
Mostly I remember how one girlfriend's father taught her to cut them

away from the root so as not to cry, and how, she'd finally told, he ate one
each night before he crept upstairs to her. Now when I smell them

in a pantry or unearth one in a field, I think of how she chopped hers
root end first, and how each time her eyes began to water.

Beauty

She wakes early with sunrise, grinds
and brews coffee, splashes it with cream.
Stands in her garden, ankles jeweled
with dew from the grass, pants rolled
to her knees. She deadheads the roses,
studies the slow growth of tomatoes and peppers.
She takes a clay pitcher, same one she'll stir
tea in later with lemons and honey,
waters the basil, bee balm and mint.
Scratches her cat's chin and belly.
He uncurls from tight comma to dash.
The wind pauses in the tulip poplar, quiet,
always quiet in the high limbs and coral blossoms
which flutter down like cocktail napkins.
She is motion but not movement,
the freight train in the distance, the hum
of the rails everywhere and nowhere at once.
The jay and the hummingbird, pale moon
still descending in morning sky, bright pollen
on her sandals, and the scent, each morning,
when she opens the door and returns,
lavender on her wrists.

In the Strip Clubs of Bluefield, West Virginia

No one's fool enough here to call them
Gentlemen's Clubs. Weeknights they're crammed
with ex-miners and railroad men smoking Salems
and drinking Pabst Blue Ribbon in a can.
Most haven't mined since '80 when they voted Reagan.
They'd rather drink than vote again.

The women are beautiful when the lights
are dim and smoke thick as valley fog.
One brunette who dances every night is scarred,
gray seam from hip to tit. It's hard not to want
to touch it. She whispers in an ear,
"Dig long and hard enough, my daddy
always said, and you'll turn up diamonds."
Still you could find love here, of a kind.

Beyond the rail yard, Victorian homes
of scrolled gingerbread decay to shades of gray.
Only the cemeteries are manicured, graves smooth
as billiard felt. That's why men arrive early
Wednesday nights. Dollars unfolded as if promised
for Baptist collection plates. Every sinner hoping
for a little extra. Why shouldn't they go down
on their knees, pray for any life beyond this one.

Desire

This is not light to wake in; this is August light, wind-borne
and sun-leached, light to worry down to its smallest exhalations.
From her hospital bed, she can see sunlight wrench the scorched limbs
of the marlberry beyond the window. She knows well these betrayals,

exposures to pain, the drainage tube in her chest, the nurse's knotted hands
rooting through meat, scraping across breastplate. Another morning
this moan might mean desire, a lover's hand brushing nipple, kissing that
bulb which will become the wintry bloom of what once was human.

Lament

Since youth's natural course is to forget
morning light soft and powdered with pollen
above the snap beans, the grandmothers swollen
with age, husking corn in August's pregnant heat,
the Louisville Slugger stabbed into riverbank, set
to mark the cottonmouth's last crossing, the call
of dusk, fall's patient longing in the laurel,
what are we to do about those boys, sons
who could not look beyond the Dog Star's horizon,
could not imagine themselves as men who reason
in waiting rooms while dying mothers groan,
their bodies pinched and tattered to the bone.
How bewildered sons become without summer's fire,
discovering grief is offspring of desire.

Detectable

Each thing we see hides something else we want to see. Rene Magritte

Every living thing does it,
peeks into the unknown: leaf-shoot and blossom
testing the great emptiness of winter,
robin angling head to ground listening
to an absence, waiting for it to reveal
the soft slither of worm-life, beetle cracking open,
sonic rapture in the earth's deep clay.
No different than the SETI astronomer casting about
in the waves and particles of deep space,
searching for a sign there's more
in that dark and light matter than the echo
of our voices. It's easy to believe
we can cavort through the universe, transported
on radio waves, conversing with whatever
or whomever we wish. Imagine those earthly broadcasts
of the 1930's radio show hurtling through the cosmos,
landing on some far world as breaking news,
or what rates as news in the cold of space,
reporting the voice of Orson Welles
delivering planetary deathblows.
Imagine those distant moons, those untouched civilizations
hearing for the first time an alien voice,
and wondering out loud
that great common denominator: "What if?"
Think about the cancer patient seeing her chest,
the ridged and puckered scar that can't help
but appear like emptied tributaries stretching
over Martian deserts, nakedness revealing

the ghost-life of the younger self.
The search exists because we need
to think there is a there, there.
We need to discover, to comprehend,
for the void to cry out
Yes, there was a before, and yes, there will be an after.
When my father called to say my mother had died,
his voice crackled across the air
from so distant a place it's as if his words,
after years of deep space travel,
were flung earthward, rejected by stars, wormholes,
and every reasoned and unreasoned creation
man's mind could fashion. We wanted to understand,
wanted to discover, even if all that existed
was the vast silence
neither of our voices could hope to fill.

Feral

Any garden will do, the one out back
where onions and asparagus ripen
in red clay. So do the ones where doe
and fawn devour suburban daisies,
manicured boxwoods. For me,
it was my mother's rose garden,
though hardly a garden, three lone plants,
stalks pruned back to stubs,
and that first green sprout
I bent to study in afternoon light
before I knew her life was over.
"Spring," she once said, "always confuses them.
How do they know it's begun and winter done?"
Even now Easter's azaleas break open
beneath a heavy sky. Things grow too quickly here.
Snow beginning to fall around red blooms,
each bud and root struggling to make sense of what to do,
the west wind shaking maples and oaks,
and my mind skittish, too, filled
with grief's wild and surprising abundance.

For the Winter Burials

I.

Rivers and streams, she said. Oceans
and seas. We all call across those waters.
This, she said, means family.

Pike, he countered, and muskie and fingerling prey
because he wasn't sure how to love.

II.

So it doesn't hurt too much
point the rifle at the temple.
Bring the ax down quickly.
Let it hang, after rubbing the ham in salt,
till spring. Then it's cured. Salt cured,
so the pain of dying is remembered.

III.

Thread the needle. Stitch the wound. Draw
the blood until the body lies
gray and cold. The corpse rose
like a moon over the smokehouse. No.
The moon rose like a corpse over the valley.
Corpse-light. Moonlight. I'm never sure.
This, I think, is how we learn to love.

IV.

"Nothing a little hard work can't cure,"
the grandfathers would say,
sipping their coffee, arguing
their yellow dog politics of the day.
But it is never enough
to labor each morning
near the meadow where sunlight drifts
through the vertebrae of trees,
to cord the oak and poplar until hands ache
beyond need for memory or forgiveness,
to drink from that brook unkinking itself
beside the graves.

V.

We want to believe
in happiness. We want to believe the trout,
hook-jawed and scarred beneath the ice,
smolder in the current.
But autumn's excess has passed without notice,
and I don't want to release your hands.
Beneath polished cliffs, the river rolls
and vanishes, and our house,
there, on that laurel-rooted hill,
holds its light against the grinding
grammar of a world that flees
while we stand still.

Omnivorous

It wasn't the sound of teeth gnawing
through plaster, nor the sound
of rat's paws nesting in the ceiling

that woke me from the dream. I heard nothing
but my own sleeping voice
rasping in the black burrow of my throat.

Always when I wake from that nightmare
it is the taste I remember,
gun powder and sulfur, the flintiness of steel.

The father snapped the bullets
into the chamber, pulled the trigger.
Dust kicked up as each rat squealed to its hole.

Standing in the garden the ravenous had ravaged,
the mother groaned, "What more?"
Her voice the sound of twigs under boot.

After each round of shots there was the calm
that accompanies failure. The broken window,
wind-bent door. Bloodied oak stump something hurried under.

In this vision they are and are not my parents. They are
older than they were at 24 when they stood cold
as sacks of seed potatoes.

Wrinkled on their foreheads, trails to a future
no more real or certain than Baptist hymns they sang
on Sunday mornings, the ones they believed

could lead them home, sate their hunger,
turn black roots and mountain loam into manna.
Always behind them their scurrying pack

of kids tore through screen doors, chewed
on knuckles and tires. They fed on anger,
bloated with the fear of being alive.

Killing

How long the bat, wing caught and twisted in a branch, waited
for a breeze to release it, I can't guess. As I read morning papers,
all seemed in order: summer storm holding off, cacophony of bikes
on gravel, wasp hunting in sweet pea vines, neighbor's cat circling the oak.

I should have thought of something tender, a pup's mouth lapping milk,
or when the good wing fluttered, imagined the fledgling flight of jays.
Instead I lifted a garden stone, crushed the skull, saw eyes fade gray.
Then I turned to headlines on Syria, stats on the Braves,
how the weather forecast called for more of the same.

The Monsters of Bomarzo

Because the hands of the deaf couple
in the gelato shop flew like falcons hunting,
I suspected all language was meant to hurt.
Arriving in Italy too late for spring,
we found mornings in the piazza retreated quickly,
leaving the cobbled alleys dumbstruck by heat.
Still, we heard voices beyond fountains,
polite breakfast conversation suffocated
by steaming pots and sliced bread drowned in oil,
bright-faced teens in the town square
performing *Medea's* death and betrayal.
Beyond the village wall carved granite faces
suggested madness in the hammer and chisel,
in the hand, in the imagination's deep shaft.
It's in the egg and sperm, in the nursery's soft sleeping,
in garden vines which pretend order
spreads over trellis and arbor.
When my childhood friend's hand fell on the trigger
all those years ago, madness was there, too,
in muscle and follicle, in the dark-tunneled throat.
I couldn't shape words to call to him.
Each sound hardened on the tongue,
discarded like half-chiseled stone.

Brodsky's Last Solstice: A Cento

If anything's to be praised, it's most likely how
In winter it darkens the moment lunch is over.
Oysters, like girls, like pearls,
A hard-boiled egg cupped by the marble cold,
Everything has its limit, including sorrow.
Autumn in your hemisphere whoops cranes and owls;
Birds acquaint themselves with leaves.
Birds don't fly through my skylight nowadays.
At sunset, when the paralyzed street gives up
Here is your frozen city cut into marble cubes.
I've been reproached for everything save the weather.
Weather wears many dresses,
While you were singing, fall arrived.
You are too young, and I am scared to touch you.
Darling, you think it's love. It's just a midnight journey.
I've seen the Atlantic,
A hotel in whose ledgers departures are more prominent than arrivals,
A bullet's velocity in low temperatures,
A stuffed quail,
Lousy times: nothing to steal and no one to steal from.
Should I say that you're dead?
The eastern tip of the empire dives into night.
As for the stars, they are always on.

Swallows at Dusk: Vitorchiano

How beautiful the broken light on the canyon,
the rock-ribbed plunge along the cliff, wind in the eyes
and the earth rising, opening to the beaked mouth.
Only in the final moment does the world turn away

and thermals, lingering over dry river bed, rise
like evening vespers to carry the day across
the western wall. Swallows huddle on night's thin wire.
The village turns silent, tucked beneath those dusky wings.

Wolf Creek Lullaby

Summer creek and autumn creek, frozen creek with sunlight chasing
minnows, silver shards of moon rocks in the shallows,
creek for toad and hawk, sleeping creek and laurel rasping creek,
boyhood waters of mist and midges, of tires and rotted rope,

creek of drowning sinners and newborn saints,
apostolic creek cleansed in bone and semen, menstruating creek,
creek of birth, of pine cone and dogwood blossom, creek of lust
and summer storm, the lightning and north wind, creek of altars
and carved sanctuary stone, creek of the blackened loam of home.

II. Selected Poems
1990–2007

Look around you. Ever is a long time. But the boy knew what he knew.
That ever is no time at all.
Cormac McCarthy, *The Road*

The Invisible Life

—Fanny Mendelssohn, 1805-1847

1. The Well-Tempered Clavier

It didn't have to be played for father's affection,
but I played it anyway. Twenty-four preludes
from memory, an ornament worn by a thirteen-year-old girl
who persevered against ambition. For what father
wants an ambitious daughter. As father said,
femininity alone is becoming in a woman.
Yet, this morning I woke to write a lied, and last week
finished another, and the week before that,
two more. I confess today while resting in the garden
I saw bees so laden with pollen my heart burst
to show the labor my own clipped wings carry.
It is easy to be ambitious. The test is not to be.

2. Lieder for Wilhelm

—Berlin 1829

The canvas aches for your brush's stroke,
the keyboard desires touch. Across the court,
Mother and Rebecka, in summer coats,
tie clematis to trellis, unaware I apprentice myself,
match my lover's sighs, duet becoming solo.

We must all learn a new language to recognize
the cadence of the husband's sleep sounds,
the thrum of chest and blood,
the length of time his body lives in darkness,
how one mouth pours across another.

Our first night, when your hand slid from my side,
how my spine vibrated with that passing,
strings on a bass quivering
in the perfect absence between breaths.
And though others object, believe what is set,

that minor is subject to major, you and I favor
the minor mode, an afternoon of Haydn,
sketch books in the garden,
the intimate view of sparrow
whose song and wing-stroke
call us to where invisible spaces open.

3. Silence

*I no longer know how it feels when one wants
to write a lied. Will the feeling return, or was
Abraham simply old?*

—Winter 1838

I don't know where to find you now
that the world offered me exhausts
itself in these few rooms,
the dry stalks of the frozen garden.
Where are the chords I woke to
as a child, the clacking of horse and carriage
down Leipziger Strasse, the orchids rasping
against the *Gartenhaus*, father's footfalls in the hall?
Piano and singing before breakfast,
cello by noon. Bach, Mozart, Haydn,
where are you, why aren't you
singing in my head? J'ai perdu
tout mon bonheur, all is lost, and my fifth finger
grows weak. You must see this is useless, silence

strengthens off those who believe they must be
all things or nothing—the bourbon rose,
the painter's wife, the brother's accompanist,
the jew, the christian. And how, brother, can I explain
to you in your world of men and music,
that here the rain on the roof falls without echo,
without rhythm, that the queen in her nest
no longer hums a song the drones follow?

4. *Sontagsmusik*

-1847

Winter draft from the window, half-light in the garden,
tea steaming on a simple table, silver spoons
in porcelain cups practicing overtures. The composer
traps the keys beneath her hands, and begins,
she believes, a song only she will know, a song
for the Prussian peasant, the exiled virtuoso,
the swallow's cry in cypress trees, the distant canals of Venice.
Her palms arch against the story behind the notes:
child prodigy, ugly daughter, hunchback, jew
who isn't a jew. What story aches behind the tongue?
Outside, cholera coats each street and alley.
Her diary becomes a mass for the dead, for the almost-dids.
But on this January Sunday, who's to say
what genius can or can't do? Who's to say that the chords
we hear aren't the wounds we live in?
No, on this day, in this half-lit garden room,
let's agree that genius just might be
the silence, the fresh cuttings arranged
on the linen-covered table, small, and unnoticed.

Products of Combustion

The neighbors said she looked holy,
a burning bush rooted in her front lawn.
A man across the street rushed
with a blanket, but the woman danced
away, twirled into the wind.

I walked to the charred grass
in the middle of her yard, a five-year-old's
crayon drawing of a black sun. Or maybe
a black swan, I thought, a migrating
black swan resting in the rigid grass.
I saw its body round and thick, a head,
and feathers fanning out.

I wanted to believe it just a trick,
an illusion where she'd appear
a dove. Perhaps she was one
of the old circus Fire Kings eating flames,
spitting water, sipping molten
lead, and cooking eggs for her son
in the greasy palm of her hand.

But knowing what I knew, how this charcoal sketch
stretched across the dried path
from doorway to street,
a thousand steps a week, how the dead
woman's husband holding the remains
of her sari, said calmly
and without fear, "Something dark and terrible
ate at her for years," I burned, amazed
at what I needed.

Revolution Begins in Persia: 1779

In Kerman, children are killing roaches,
just as their mothers asked.
They shake them from their bedrolls,
stomp them with bare feet,
and leave smeared husks. These the mothers
sweep into sand and dust. Then the beds are rolled back neatly,
lined and stacked beneath a window.
Pottery is washed, rewashed, and scrubbed.

After all the village houses are straightened,
each family member doused with water
bourne daily from a stream, the children
line up with their parents
along the only village street: a parent, a child,
each family repeats the sequence until it ends.
Up front, the soldiers' swords leap about
like snared fish. Parents flop on the ground.
The image is welded on the children's eyes
with the blinding tips of knives.

The Agha Kahn's soldiers continue until evening,
when even with rest, some food and drink,
they haven't the strength to finish. At the end
of the line, a mother and boy are left untouched,
unmoved by threats they'll be first tomorrow.
One soldier tries to throw his sword,
hoping fear will cut as deep as metal.
It falls at the child's feet.
The boy looks into the man's eyes and knows
what the soldier doesn't know: fear,
during the wait, was cleansed from his chest.

Later, with no time to grieve,
the mother and boy begin picking up again.
Miles away the egg of a storm cracks open,
a swirl of wind a child's hand might make.
Patiently it grows, an hour, a day,
a year, two hundred years until the sun
has vanished. When it's finished
all of Persia is stripped clean.

from *Original Sins*

III. Giordano Bruno at the Inquisition

It isn't the heavens, or loneliness, I tell you.
It's the view from my cell window, the prismatic lilacs
in the unmown field, a constellation of cobblestones
covered with dung, night staining the worlds' apocryphal
four corners in spite of the moon. The Ptolemaic soul
exists in a static state while we flounder
in our muddied fish bowl adrift in a dark sea.
Observe how one system becomes another, how
servants become builders, builders become soldiers
who become priests, and all become judges and judged.
Kill me and a thousand worlds continue circling a thousand stars
where an infinitude of rodents scurry content in their ignorance,
accepting grace beneath the torch's sting. If we believe
this human condition remains merely human, then it is
impossible to stare at the stars and not be destroyed.

Arguing Exile

In Pulawy only the horses knew where they were going.
Their hooves recited the cobbled streets
while in our apartment we confined love
to small words of thrust and dodge. Silence reduced
to corners recanting the world's extremes.
That night in the shadows of the streetlamp,
an old woman, scarf tight around her face,
knotted hands flashing in light
like scythes through grass, motioned me near.
Uncertain if she were sick, or lost,
or as scared of the world as I was,
I rushed home through that country I hardly knew,
streets I'd never walked, that town where night
smoldered strangely above the skyline,
to where my wife sealed in sleep
dreamed of horses near her grandfather's yard,
and a time when, *who is my husband?*
who is my wife? were questions we didn't need to ask,
when moonlight urged bodies together, when the irregular
chime of reins, the imagined loneliness of horses
shackled to carts, their companionship with stones,
had not crossed into this human language.

With Susan in Krakow

In a square that's echoed a thousand times the priest's
confessions, the soldier's polished steps, we locate
the echo of our waking. Hungry, thirsty, filled with an empty ache

we've carried from Oswiciem's haunted barracks, we've risen
early leaving behind yesterday to find sunlight
hanging like bright scarves in the alleys.

Only simple pleasures today. Coffee in a white porcelain cup,
cakes filled with berries and nuts, a fresh linen napkin, ice in a glass.
When the trumpets blow from St. Mary's tower, we want to believe

no one hears this but us. Barely married, unseasoned, we've lived
less than the market fruit stands, the grapes rushed to wine,
the grasses bent to baskets. Yet here we are

a snapshot coloring to bright reds and distant greys,
no sepia, only the memorable our lives exist in now,
a city so filled with what's been, we hardly see the future.

Negative Space

My wife is drawing the body
as best she can, dark line
against the blankness she now has
a name for. She has always felt it,
that empty hole we live
our lives filling. What she's after
is winter's blood & heart, the solid heft
of breath steaming across the mouth,
frozen, measurable, ecstatic.

Insomnia

The way, from 30,000 feet, the earth
      looks like marble, or sorghum swirled
in a batter, beaten and mixed up,
      this is how it is in the beginning
of the middle of the night.
      We think we need miracles
but it doesn't have to be
      parachutes opening, or the chemistry of yeast.
Why not my life as sawdust
      layered over a concrete floor, or the muddied
light of rain puddled in a footprint,
      or an olive ground into white linen?
How can we resist waking?
      The night is a lie whispered
in our ears, the breath perfumed
      with the scent of fresh peaches
and only a hint of hurt in the hard, bitter pit,
      a dark bruise rooted in light.

Gravity

The two a.m. face of the waitress rising
over a steaming pot of boiling beans
in an all-night diner near Hays, Kansas;
the well-fed hawk resting on power lines;
the astronauts of Apollo, of my childhood,
playing games in zero G's with floating Jell-O and ballpoint pens;
Skylab--both in orbit and freefalling into the Pacific;
my first lover buoyed above me, the weight of her breast
on my mouth, her wrists thin and brittle as birds' wings;
the brute whack of a Barry Bonds homerun;
the scar on my father's chest where they'd opened his ribs,
the weight of the human heart a mere 11 ounces;
the theories of Newton and Einstein, the theories
of my friend Steve on theories, how everyone's got one,
and how theories on force and resistance pushed Steve
over the mountain where, according to witnesses,
his car soared twenty feet before arcing
downward into the cliffs; James Dean;
the implosive spirals of Elvis, Jimi Hendrix and Kurt Cobain;
the coal-blackened faces of miners near Logan, West Virginia
stepping from the mountain's shaft into moonlight;
Hunter, at three, calling out, "Be careful. You'll fall like an angel,"
and me surprised that he knew that phrase,
so surprised I start to say how it's too late,
Daddy's already fallen. But I think he won't get the joke.
Those Sunday rides as a kid in my Dad's Caprice convertible;
how the leaves on the maple and oak flared in the sunlight,
the way the limestone cliffs, solid and sheer, rose above us,
while below the gem-studded New River shimmered and shimmied;
the way my Dad always took the same highway,
the way his loose curls flew around his face like a boy's,
how he laughed and reached to hold my mother's hand,

the way she smiled back and breathed easily,
the wind carrying us to no particular destination,
only the hum of the engine and the thumping mantra of the road;
how the following day we'd rush to work and school
and clean house and pay bills while the air around us would sizzle
with arguments and fear, betrayals without forgiveness;
how for a few hours every Sunday there was the road,
and those first evening stars reflected in the river;
and of course there's always the river forced lower and deeper,
and dawn the color of bruised gills,
and the fishermen stalking the trout, casting the cricket into eddies
so it dances just enough to lure the fish to surface
because the trick, you see, is not to cast a shadow,
the trick is to believe we're made of light,
and we've never really fallen.

Blind–Sided

Only one person is known to have been hit by
a meteorite. On November 30, 1954, Mrs. E.H. Hodges
of Sylacauga, Alabama, was sitting in her house after
lunch when a 9-pound stone crashed through the roof
and hit her on the thigh.—Walter Sullivan, *We Are Not Alone*

Nine years and three days later I drop to the earth
with considerably less speed, but with as great
an impact, or at least that's how my mother tells it.
And she lived to tell about it, as did Mrs. Hodges,
once she recovered from the shock, the thrill
of coming as close to the eternal universe, eternally,
as a few inches. But isn't that always the way.
One moment we're minding our own business,
wandering about in our lives, no apparent course,
the next we're rolling diapers into a meteoric knot
and hurling them into the pail.
Or, as with my friend J., we're finishing
our lunch when out of nowhere a wife stiffens in her seat
and looks across the room. There's nothing there,
but still she looks, hoping that the words will fall
from the heavens. There is no easy way
to say it, so she leans into the table
and without apology says she's had enough,
that it's her turn to find herself, that the monotonous
orbit she's been forced into won't do. Her tight, stony fists
hang in her lap. Silences stretch light years,
and all the feeble attempts at reconciliation
will never reach her now. It's the same feeling
as when Mark Preston blind-sided me,
stone-hard knuckles snapped the ridge of my nose,
a stream of blood flared into the parking lot.

Some other kid might have swung back, but I was horrified
at the pool filling my palm. *My blood*,
I repeated to myself as I sat there
quietly while a friend finished off the guy I believed
was trying to finish me. He never knew what hit him.
Nor did Mrs. Hodges until they calmed her, medicated
her from a pain that wouldn't end. Years later she'd wake
to the fiery ache in her leg, a reminder of what she'd
been and what she'd become, survival's gravity
twisting her life into one deep breath, like the first breath
that coughs up the phlegm of another world and deposits
it right here in this one where all around us stars
flare into bits of battered stone, and the universe
leaves each of us alone to explode in all directions.

Devolution Theory

Late at night when I remember the women
who shaped their lips into a perfect "O"
over the burning end of a joint and blew
shotguns into my mouth until our heads
grew as full of static as the AM station
out of Dubuque and we slid naked and willing
into the backseat, I'm amazed I've ended up
this marginally respectable, 401K contributing,
family man. I'm as likely to be caught
today reading *Popular Science* on a park bench.
Or if I'm really daring, you might find me browsing Darwin
at Hot Rodz, the local exotic bar, where $4.50 buys you
a watered-down bourbon and a corner table
far enough back not to be bothered or recognized
but close enough, between paragraphs, to watch the dancers.
There are moments when I allow myself these visits
into the smoke and light of my former life
that I hear my name denounced through the megaphone
of what's correct and decent,
and I rush outside to make certain no one
is photographing my car and license plate
for distribution on the Web under the title
"Perverts and Miscreants of the Carolinas."
It isn't that I've forgotten my wife,
or the women before her I spent whole nights with
arguing the rules of love. I wouldn't
exchange a single one of them for any
locker room myth-fest or testosterone prom.
But I won't renounce that world of men either,
leaning against their Mustangs and pickup trucks,
their hoods lifted like battle flags,
groping beers and engines as readily as anything,

sniffing the exiled edge of a wilderness of their own making.
Maybe this is the best that natural selection can do.
Marking trees and tires with our own pee's scent,
barking out lists of boasts, we dream of wading mouth-
deep in the slough of primordial love, not because we're afraid
to hope for something finer, but because we see
those invisible borders drawn on bodies,
places allowed and forbidden, and growing closer
we hear the robotic clamoring of the soul.
So like any good primate we thrust a hand deep
into the stinging ant's hill because what's hidden there
tastes sweet, and the pain, being this much
alive, sweeter still.

Physics 101: Principia Corporis

Sir Isaac Newton never made love.
Overheard in Nick's Bar

A body in motion remains in motion
she recited down the stairs, and out my door.
Going, I understood, was what we knew best:
the flicker of quarks, the orbit of atoms
combining to make the finger that waved me off.
In a simpler time we could believe
that if you knew the condition, you'd know the result.
Now, I'm told that every reaction between
a quantum event and an observer,
trillions of which are happening as you read this,
splits the cosmos into billions of universes.
And in one, Isaac Newton peers out his window as the women
of 1687 browse the markets, hurry to lunch, to parties,
cross his street, pass his door,
and keep solidly in their paths, always.
Later, Newton, naked and alone with his compass
and calipers deciphering the world to its abstract equation,
looks up to the building across from his at the silhouette
of a man pulling a woman close, a chiaroscuro
of light particles and shadow waves commingling
until the universe, extended its billion times,
shrinks to the confines of two bodies.

Quantum Flux

It's easy to believe they didn't exist, but they were
us. Even now, that day's light is carried
its 186,000 miles per second: two potential lovers
standing on a bridge above the Arkansas River, revealing
themselves in ways they can't predict: the shy one
proving how she could spit as well as any man, and the other,
the doubter, believing her capable of anything she wished. In physics

there's a place for this, a quantum moment between cause
and effect when anything can happen. In Schrödinger's box
the cat is either alive or dead; between the notes
silence exists eternal or another sound rings out.
When a marriage starts there is no certainty. We guess
at love's results. Since that moment on the bridge,
we're living and waiting in a wave.

Lunar Cartography

I love the places on the moon
that remind me of your body.
Mare Nectaris, the shadow of your neck,
Mare Vaporum, deep valley of your spine.
Exiled places where touching leaves no trace.
Like the trout we caught, cold, foreign;
their scales a flat, reflected light
across the lake. Or the beggar in Krakow
who questioned us in words we couldn't
live in. Yet her hands and her flute sang like wrens
in apple trees. Their eyes, like yours, fixed
not on the stars, but on the wind, the stones,
the moon's flame in black vines.

American Love: Archeological Style

There's little that can't be found,
valued or lost, including love,
in the middle of the Sam's Super Warehouse.
The great American machine pumps out more
tires, tents, candies, chips and cellophaned meats
than my gluttonous eyes can scan. I spend
whole mornings rummaging in bins of batteries,
baskets of breads (European crusty and traditional
sandwich white), racks of cleaning fluids,
disposable razors, diapers, and baby wipes.
Or I'll investigate the discounted books and magazines,
best-sellers, sci-fi, low-fat cookbooks, tomes on ancient
Egyptian dynasties and the burial rituals of the pyramids.
Most days I need no reason to browse,
but this morning after an argument
too large for words hours ago,
now too small to remember,
I'm here searching for some token
to show it's possible for me to recognize
the many strata where love lies hidden.
Disposable gestures are my specialty.
Just last week, cleaning out a closet,
I came across the first such gift, a child's
wading pool meant to calm the waters.
It's not that I'm cheap or indifferent.
Any one can bring home roses,
or tie a ribbon around a diamond
as big as your thumb,
but who wouldn't forgive a man
offering up remorse as a turtle-shaped pool?
Admittedly, it's garbage now, or at best fodder

for next month's yard sale,
but bury it in the back yard for a thousand years
and who can guess its worth?
As my friend the collector likes to say,
one man's trash is another man's treasured artifact.
And if I'm ever dug up, what, if anything, will I reveal?
Will I be worth more than the fillings
rattling in my well-preserved jaw?
Will the salt from my last supper preserve
those Big Macs and fries for a study
on the eating habits of the extinct American middle-class?
Or like some lesser Egyptian pharaoh
will I be enshrouded by my modest trinkets:
Happy Meal toys, greeting cards, quality paperbacks
printed on acid-free paper?
Will those doctoral candidates brushing clay
from my eye sockets think I've seen
little worth recording? I admit I'm no Incan
mummy child sacrificed to the mountain gods of Peru
but I want to believe I'm something
more than the sum of bones they'll excavate.
I'd like to think we all have stories,
no matter how chain-store common,
to form a future that won't deny us.
Today, I've purchased an apple peeler
and some Autumn Harvest incense
from the half-price barrel.
I'll apologize to my wife
and try not to make any grand promises.
I'll keep it simple, maybe a dinner
of corn held with those dime-store, cob-shaped skewers,
and a caramel apple pie for dessert.
Then, satisfied, we'll sleep, and wake
to one of those days I value most

when I brush the sleep from her eyes,
and we take all morning to unbury ourselves
from sheets and blankets. Mornings when we linger
over one another, if we're lucky,
like ruins longing to be discovered.

Casualties

I still remember you, Howard Pancake,
darting out to pump the gas,
all bobbing head and hands
like twitching hounds. Shakes
from the war, my father said,
who was still young enough
to call you sir when you talked of weather,
how late the snow held on,
how crops would fall to ruin
if the season didn't turn.
I remember how your voice
stammered like machine gun fire
and your eyes flew from corner
to corner wary of surprise,
and how Bobby Jones once called you hero
because you'd saved three men
from a mortar attack in France.
Never the same after, he said.
Even in your sleep you heard
the blast of splintered rock and bone.
When I played war in the woods
by Bluestone Creek on trails
Confederate soldiers marched
one hundred years before, I pretended
I was braver than you, an old man
shackled with shakes and shivers. I saved
a dozen, more, a whole platoon,
drawing down with steady gaze
and steady hands on hidden foes.
In '68, when they listed Bobby's father
killed in action, the whole town
turned out to pay respect.

You walked in late, and though I'm sure
your hands still shook, all I saw
was church-light captured in ribbons
and medals on Marine dress blues.
Outside the strafe of truck exhaust
sent quakes down necks and spines
and broke our silence.
You reached to calm Mrs. Jones,
knelt by Bobby, and whispered something
to them both. Next day, over morning papers
and news of war, people guessed
at what you'd said. Something about heroes
and risk, most thought, and the will to fight.
But I doubted it, for I saw
the two black trenches of your eyes,
and even now, I hear your faltering voice
like the blind stumbling up bright stairs,
and I imagine you spoke of love and loss,
and how no matter when the season turns,
there's no acceptable sacrifice.

Lessons in Discarding

I. What Our Fathers Taught

In the summer's afternoon furnace, sons
stand off kicking stones down dirt roads,
eyes dark as veins of coal their fathers load
in Buchanon County mines. Always the entering
into the earth, and only sometimes the rising out.
The boys want none of this. They hide behind the barn,
smoke Salems, tease the rat snake from its clutch
of eggs, then stamp the shells, a yolk-phlegmed mud.
And like the snake, they feel earth's fissures quake,
father-voices rumbling underground. Mountains,
scars of the upheaval, rise, reduced to human grief.
Given time, rivers shift and leave their banks.
Sons think this loneliness. Fathers call this love.

II. What Our Mothers Taught

They gather on painted porches stringing beans
in heat thick enough to coat a spoon.
Two baskets, equally full, centered
between the women and children. One for what's kept
and canned against bleak winter. The other,
husk and stem, mulch for the spring.

Thermals

Sundays, when I was nine, we watched men disappear
into the sky, hang-gliders flying toward the Carolinas.
Less men than air, their buckles and loops chimed.
Even the steps they took, four quick steps before they threw
themselves over the cliffs, left no prints.
For a moment, my mother watched them
as they dropped below the edge,
when all we heard were trees scratching gliders.
She might have thought of my father rubbing her shoulders,
wings he called them, or she might have
looked across the valley and seen a glimpse
of the nights he'd disappear and how years later
by his bed, only she would stay with him through the night.
Or perhaps it was something as simple as the kites
we'd make later with brown paper and twine
and how no matter what we tried they never flew.
Watching my mother, I understood for the first time
the battles fought between gravity and flight.
For I saw her hold her breath as if it were
all she had left, as if by warming it beneath her breasts
she might release enough to give the gliders lift.
Each time one soared into view, my mother
breathed again. They flew all afternoon.

Outlaws

This list of malefactors who become Saints in the church is long and strangely persuasive...
Albert Goldbarth

My father ran moonshine, corn whiskey,
white lightning, Devil's Rum, from Bramwell
through Bluefield to Bland, or so his story
goes. Though, when young, I never heard him tell
of such dangers, never saw him load up
the old GTO, run the serpentine ridge
of Rt. 52, fishtail Brushy Mountain, rip
open the sky, hanging to its razored edge.
Still, it's nice to imagine some outlaw gene
passed down the branches of the family tree.
So when my own life, impotent and lean
from the heart's petty thefts, hungers, I'll plea
to bandit gods, ruined brawlers and boot-leggers,
glass packs blasting, and hell to pay.

Bluefield Breakdown

Where are you Clyde Moody, and you Elmer Bird,
"Banjo Man from Turkey Creek," and you Ed Haley,
and Dixie Lee singing in that high lonesome way?
I feel the shadow now upon me...
Come you angels and play those dusty strings.
You ain't gonna work that sawmill Brother Carter,
nor sleep in that Buchanon County mine. Clawhammer
some of that Cripple Creek song. Fiddle me a line
of "Chinquapin Hunting." *Shout little Lulie, shout, shout.*
I need to hear music as lonesome as I am,
I need to hear voices sing words I've forgotten.
This valley's much too dark now.
Sunset right beside us, sunrise too far away.
I haven't heard a tipple creak all day,
and everyone I loved left
on the last Norfolk & Southern train.

Autumn in the Blue Ridge

Adrift in the garden's last Byzantine upswell:
no work, no obligation, no duty.
Only the percussion of the woodpecker
on the unyielding oak, the garish cardinal,
a single flame against hard frost,
the fattened squirrel filching acorns
from its neighbor. Occasionally,
the season's last worker bee, thin-winged
and laboring, rifles through the ripened holly,
berries mustering on fallen leaves. Without warning,
I begin to tap my feet, soaring in this thinning light
of possibility, the hunter moon hiding
behind its web of trees, the north wind a hymn
the world hums on its way to dying.

Homecoming

The choice is never wide and never free.
Elizabeth Bishop

It is always September here, summer's crops
hardening into stalks, watering cans, chalk-dry,
left to tarnish. Off Route 460, the town's only factory
stands abandoned. Its weathered smokestack spires
toward the sun; while below, the tractor meant to mow
thistle idles, cast off to the side of the road. Children,
who played hide-n-seek in hedges, vanished years ago.
Front yard deer caught grazing have turned
to stone. Even the jays and cardinals are snapshots,
frozen on concrete, garden bowls. The whole scene
antiqued for auction, for militants who shape
their lives into museums. I tell myself

leaving cost me nothing, but I know that isn't true.
These meadows of wind stained blue and green
with chicory and apple wood, reveal this
is as good a place as any to learn the language
of undoing. I've returned in the middle of this life filled
with doubt and indecision, to witness the end of a town.
Like it or not, the world answers us by discarding what we covet.
Old friends grow bald as babies. Former festival queens,
donning make-up thick as frosting on cakewalk cakes,
can't hide the fact they outlived fame. I forget the names
of streets and find the ones I do remember
won't lead me out. Like memory, they spiral and tangle
until all that's left are maps revealing how far we have to travel.

Midlothian

This far north the sun barely rises
above the horizon. It's a strange,
November day in Scotland, clear sky,
frost sent hiding, and though I need to work
I'm cutting firewood after breakfast
knowing tonight the flames will fill the room
with brandy-colored light. I am living alone,
my wife and son across the North Atlantic,
and for the first time in weeks
I'm not afraid. Even the fleet-winged hawk
high above the hare seems more graceful
than severe. Joy for both is that moment
in the field, bright noon and shadow-free,
before the talon strikes.
I kick a stone down the yew-draped path.
A limb the size of my arm drops
into the river, and out of nowhere
the sky turns gray and rain begins to fall.
Too soft, I think. Too tender.
I find the heart ripped out by claws
less offensive than the slow wearing away
that takes its toll. Give me flash floods
and lightning bolts, but not the patient
brook carving canyons in the glen.
There is no happiness in almost.
Memory's filled with what we think
we've lived. Give me absolutes.
Give me the split atom and the big bang.
Give me the racing heart,
the hawk upon my chest, those two black eyes
the universe sent forth at its beginning,
and that great empty fist,
a flash against an iron sky.

High Lonesome

It's the hammered notes of rainwater over dry October;
lost voices conjured from the polished grain of poplar,
the mandolin's tight strings pressed into the memory of wood.
It's the song of wind in laurel, the shifting sun above the chicory of June.
Song of the banjo, sweet loss thumb-picked and bone-strummed.
Songs we don't hear so much as know in heartbeat,
toe-tap, and blood-thrum. Songs hummed in kitchens and bedrooms,
in backseats rollin' in our sweet baby's arms.
Songs of pickups at dusk turning home, the AM radio broadcasting
light on the blackened faces of men heavy with the work of grief.
Songs of the barbed wire fence, the salt-cured sow,
the chicken coop, the stray hound.
Song shaped by hands breathing over gut-string and hog-hide.
Songs of towns whose names imply they might hold light.
Song of stone and storm, weary hymn of the woman
above the ironing board, the shucked corn,
the straw-haired child dancing 'round the apron strings.
Song of creek-cut valley, wind-hewn ridge. Song of the Chevy
abandoned to thistle, the plow gouging the wet pasture.
Ballad of the worm working the heart's deep cave, the shrill a cappella
of starlings in a winter field, wind on a timbered hillside,
the owl offering the half-eaten world on a bed of bones.
Songs that fill the sky above rail yards
with the scrolled promises of falling stars.

Summer, If It Ends At All, Ends Here

Sunset is lodged like a shard of glass
in the western sky. The day's heat
is pared down to something nearly benign.
Tomatoes on the vine swell deep red;
I pick one, juice spilling down my chin,
sweet acid on the tongue and throat.
Along the fence, rudbeckia towers over
the concrete bath where mocking birds
dip their heads and wings
then beat the air to smithereens.
The backyard is in a freefall.
The streetlamp releases its cone of light,
and what's veiled and unveiled enters me.
Coltrane, from the apartment next door,
blows *Giant Steps* so each breath suffers
to sound both wrong and right.
500 miles away, my mother's malignant
body sleeps after treatments,
hoping poison can kill poison.
Nothing beautiful about that healing,
the sores that open and swallow her up,
a remedy consumed with waste.
This is one kind of loneliness.
Another starts as muffled thunder
across the street before shouts and fists
spill out the screened door:
"I'll kill you, goddammit. I'll kill you."
The man's voice snaps at the woman
like a match to flame,
and the way the wind carries it,
a dry rasp over the scorched earth,
tells me he meant every word.

Dinosaurs

They're still here, only
in microscopic form: the red velvet mite,
the wingless flea leaping many times its height,
bacteria whose Latin names blend
into one inescapable snare, and now, I'm told,
to consider Martian rods, dark microbial forms
of both inner earth and outer space,
and all of these no less frightening to me
than the *Jurassic Park*-induced clones
the neighbor's kid hopes one day to recreate.
I don't want to overstate the case,
but I really do hate them, fear them crawling in my bed,
mites feeding on my body ash, lurking in the ductwork.
There are those even smaller, subsurface dwellers
starved of sunlight, carving out lives
in volcanic vents, deep mines, Antarctic ice,
feeding off sulfur, iron, radioactivity
from the earth's deep core, breeding over eons
until now their mass is greater than all of ours.

Right now the only ones I'm worried with are building
nests in the caves of my mother's lungs and breasts.
Their kind have been doing this, devouring
the body's sweetbreads, at least since the Cretaceous.
And this is why I find myself curled in my mother's room.
Great beasts click with pleasure over that body
which loved a man, bore five children, and longed
for something more than this fanged and grunting kingdom.
Below the hospital window, mowers prowl and gorge
luxurious lawns. Even the trees bend to plea
against such savagery. Each of us hoping
for the sweet ignorance to dream
the dreams of predators and not of prey.

Grief

The uncertainty in what is certain,
    the way heat phantoms off a blackened highway
rise in such distorted acrobatics
    the imagined horizon bears little resemblance
to the real curve we're hurtling toward.

Once, driving east, all those I loved still alive,
    I found a dog dead outside Tulsa blocking the way.
When I stopped to lift him to the grassy mound,
    the wound, clear to the spine, boiled with maggots.
All the way home, I imagined how by week's end
    he'd be bones, spiked and hardened to the sun.

Bird of Prey

for Hunter

Already wounds accumulate: you wake crying
out your four-year-old's screech for the owl
that, in the dark, searches yellow-eyed, dragging
the invisible through the mid-air silence,
the wing beat of stars; while just below
your temple, in that softest of flesh, a small scar
from a cut I'd never noticed rises fresh
in the talon-track of moonlight across your bed,
and catches, briefly, those ancient shadows vying
to soar into this world to strike us down,
so we may rise, not in despair,
but with the gift of day's bright pain.

Toward Any Darkness

It returns, that dream of predatory flight,
soaring above dusk light, claiming little,
maybe the corn snake I'd thought lucky
shedding one body to live in another.
I rise, quiet, camouflaged, becoming one
of those middle-aged men
who watch from safe distances.
The great bird shreds the flesh,
drives its beak into the sinew
of something rank. The offal
ushered and unraveled
like Sunday morning's first hymn,
the notes beautiful and terrible all at once,
and the sweat on the preacher's brow
rising from some place unmentionable,
deep in the blind rookery of the body.
How do I keep the violence in?
Instinct moves me to smell the blood
and bone, hear the muscles' black
roots snapped from joints.
I fear nothing can weigh me down,
keep me from understanding
how this life I craft
could have been different,
could have been more
than bric-a-brac in a cupboard.
I step back from the window.
Wind rattles the outer walls.
In the fireplace flue, the wing-flutter
of startled wrens. Shadows,
roused from the boundaries,
stir toward any darkness.

Why I Believe in Angels

Because I've seen their musculature joined
hip to hip in parked cars, their bones,
under the glisten of skin, twisting into flight.
Because I've seen them rock through one another
in that oldest of nights, in that moonless hour of clarity
when the field mouse briefly turns its head from danger
and only a wing beat marks its passing.

Because I've heard them speak in tongues
in late night bars as their bodies writhed
in the stage's strobed light. Because I've seen
their breasts encircled in the incense of cigarette,
and I've held their heart's beating planchette and deciphered
scribbled prophecies on back-alley walls and discovered
their words, like ours, are mere ticks on a clock.

Because I believe the quark and lepton that leap from lover's mouths
were once part of a rotting branch on Centauri Prime,
and because I wake at night full of a past compressed beside me,
the voices of friends whose wives left or husbands cheated,
who, faced with such truths, are certain they didn't know:
"I stood there," they confess, "though someone else possessed my body."
Then all I can imagine are the unpaid bills a life accumulates,
the voracious guilts and minor misdemeanors, the interpenetration
of morphogenetic fields that allows the rat in Seattle to convey
the way through the maze to a rat in Boston to the rat inside my head,
and because I can't ignore these signs, because I can't ignore,
I find, without looking or understanding, my wife's hands,
or my son's hands, crossed upon my chest,
and there like two wings they've ended their journey.

Notes

Monsters of Bomarzo: The Park of Monsters in the Garden of Bomarzo was commissioned in 1552 by Prince Pier Francesco Orsini as an expression of the Prince's grief.

Brodsky's Last Solstice: Each line in the poem is a first line from a poem by Joseph Brodsky quoted from *Collected Poems in English*

Music Theory and *Bird of Prey* are for Hunter.
Hunger Ghazal and *Beauty* are for Susan.

And a little something in each of these exists for my parents who encouraged me to love books.

Rick Mulkey is the author of four previous poetry collections, including *Toward Any Darkness, Before the Age of Reason, and Bluefield Breakdown.* Individual poems and essays have appeared in a variety of periodicals such as *Crab Orchard Review, Denver Quarterly, The Literary Review, Poet Lore, Poetry East, Shenandoah,* and *Southern Poetry Review*, and his work has appeared in numerous anthologies, including *American Poetry: the Next Generation, The Southern Poetry Anthology: Volumes I and II,* and *A Millennial Sampler of South Carolina Poetry*, among others. He has received a Hawthornden Fellowship and *The Literary Review*'s Charles Angoff Award, among others. Mulkey has taught at universities and writing workshops in the United States and Europe, and he currently directs the low residency MFA program in Creative Writing at Converse College.

CPSIA information can be obtained
at www.ICGtesting.com
Printed in the USA
LVOW12s0547010318

568198LV00009B/1126/P